Cartoons by Tim Whyatt
All images ©Tim Whyatt 2002-2017

Published by Studio Press
An imprint of Kings Road Publishing. Part of Bonnier Publishing
The Plaza, 535 King's Road, London, SW10 0SZ

www.bonnierpublishing.co.uk

Printed in Italy   10 9 8 7 6 5 4 3 2

SENIOR MOMENTS

Love & Marriage

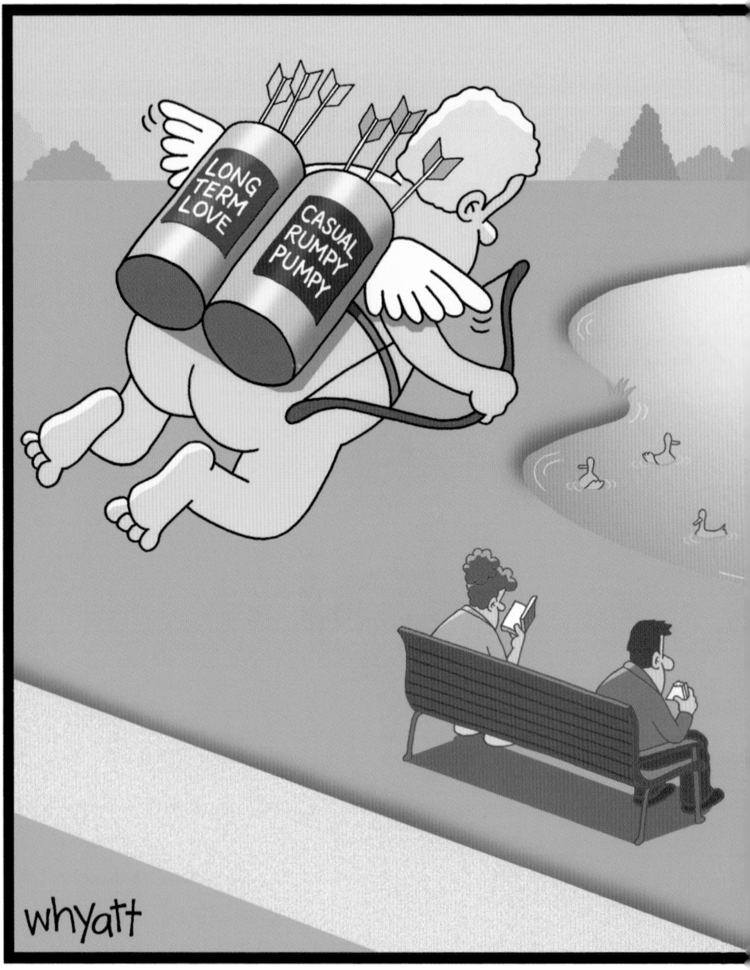
LONG TERM LOVE
CASUAL RUMPY PUMPY
whyatt

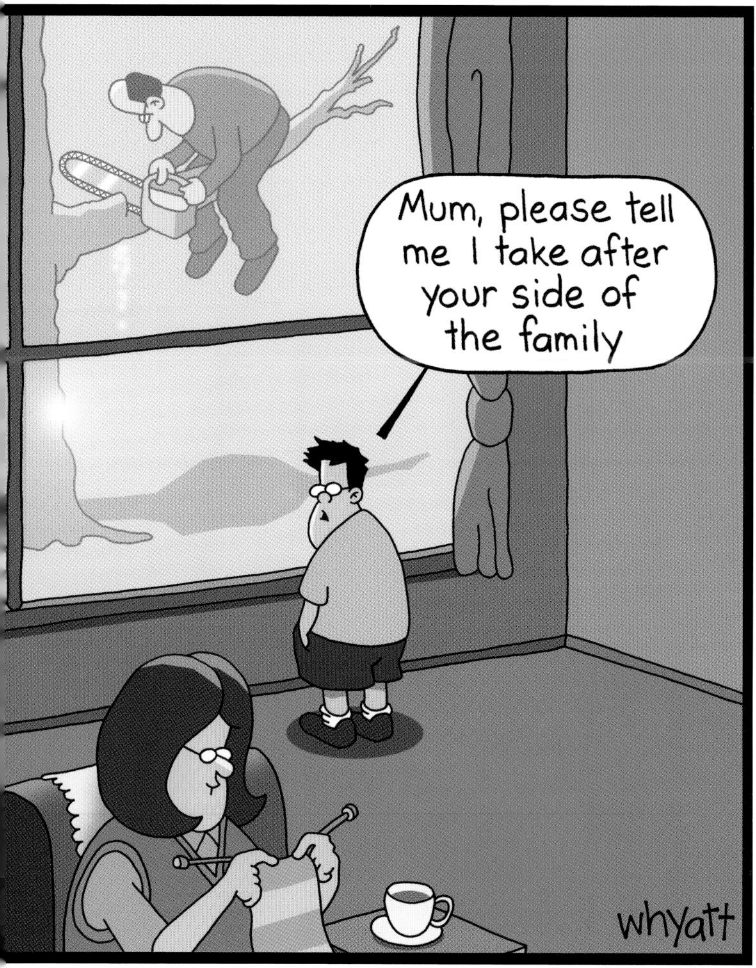
Mum, please tell me I take after your side of the family
whyatt

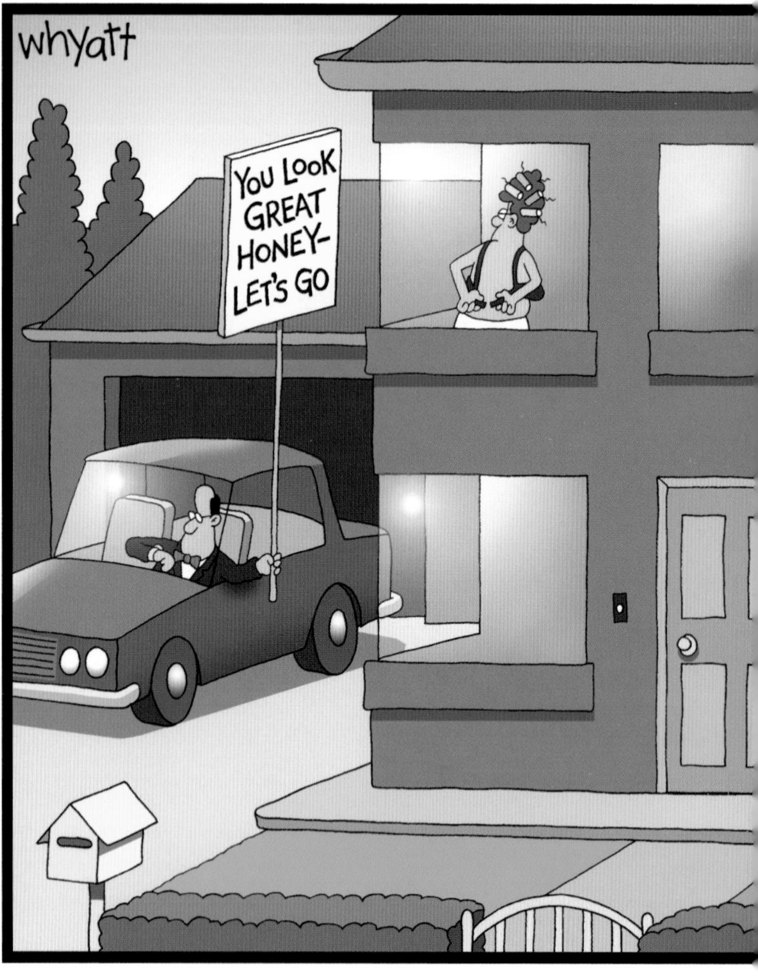
whyatt
YOU LOOK GREAT HONEY- LET'S GO

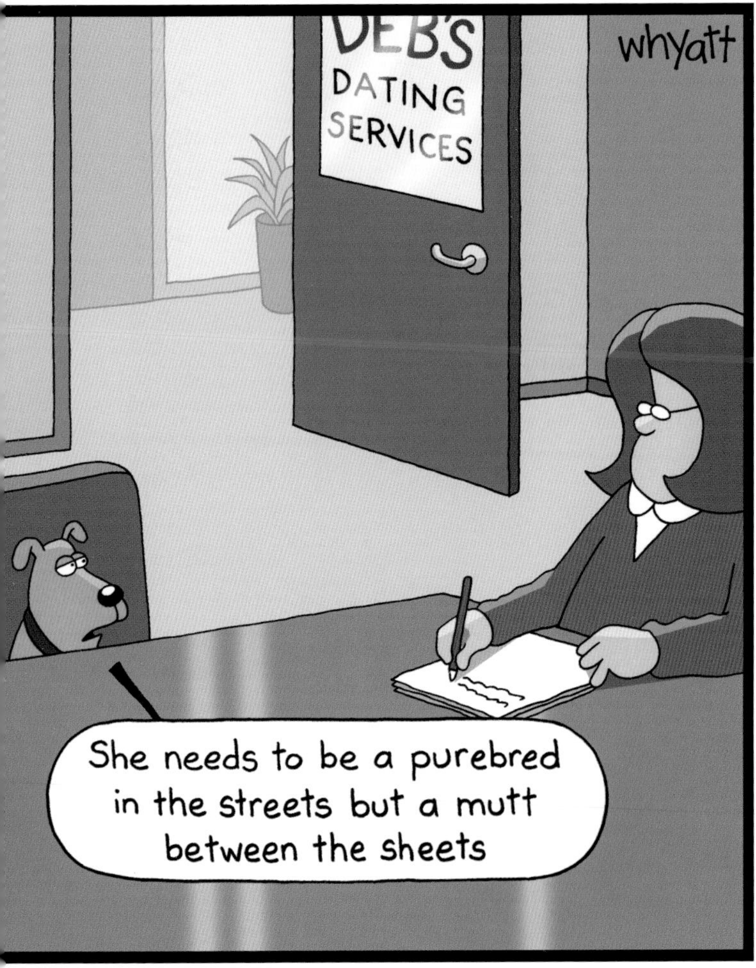
DEB'S
DATING
SERVICES
whyatt
She needs to be a purebred in the streets but a mutt between the sheets

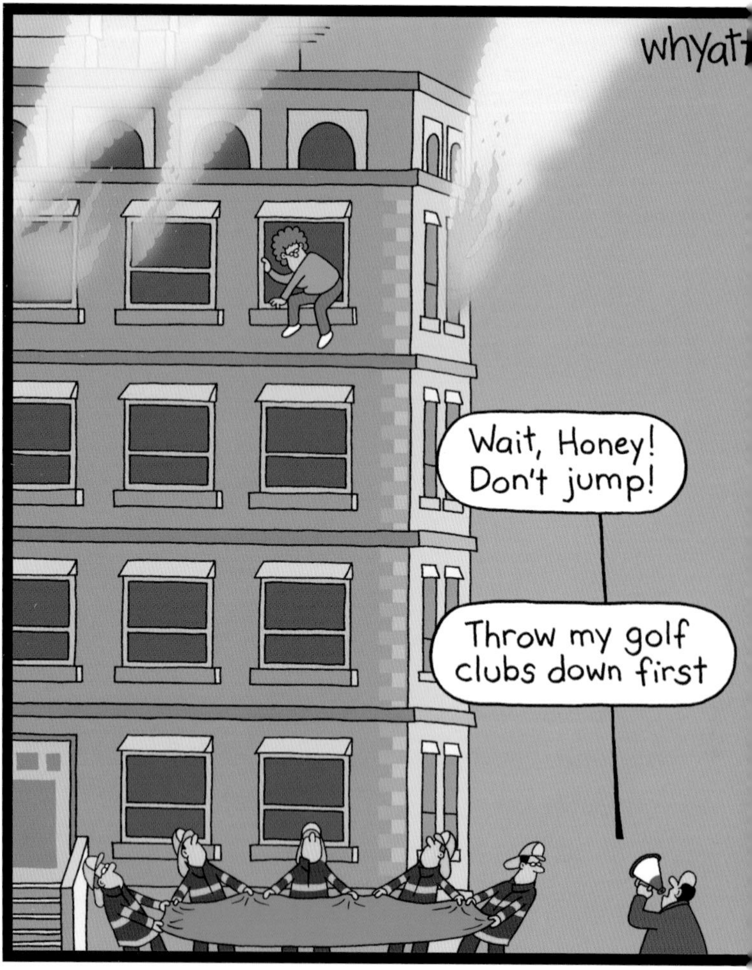
whyatt
Wait, Honey! Don't jump!
Throw my golf clubs down first

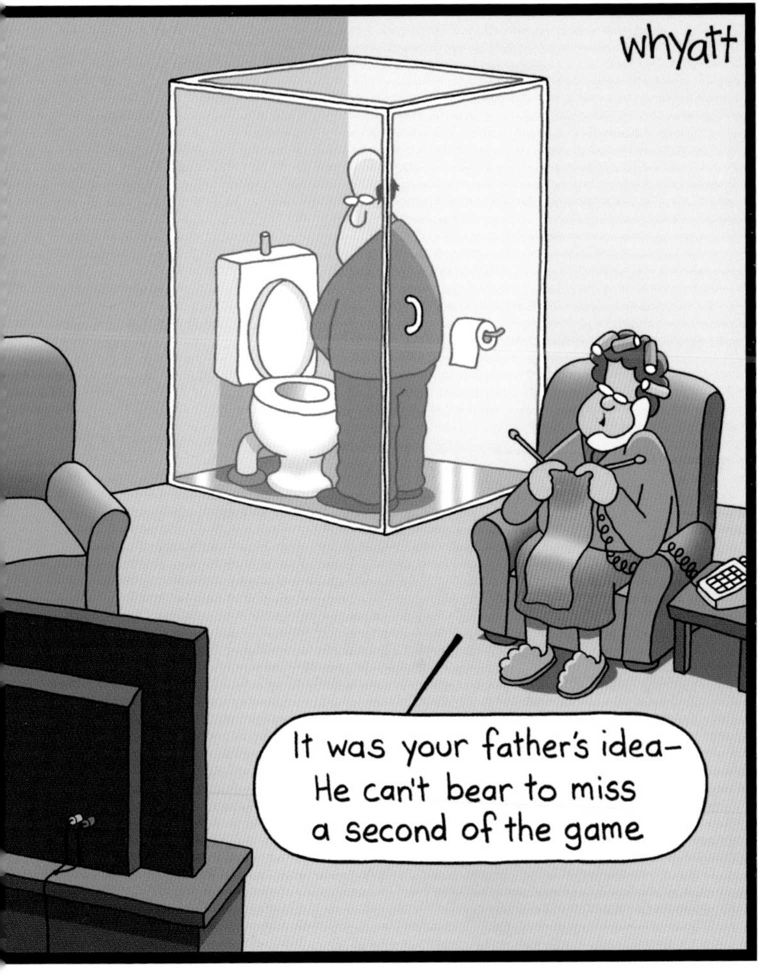
whyatt
It was your father's idea-
He can't bear to miss
a second of the game

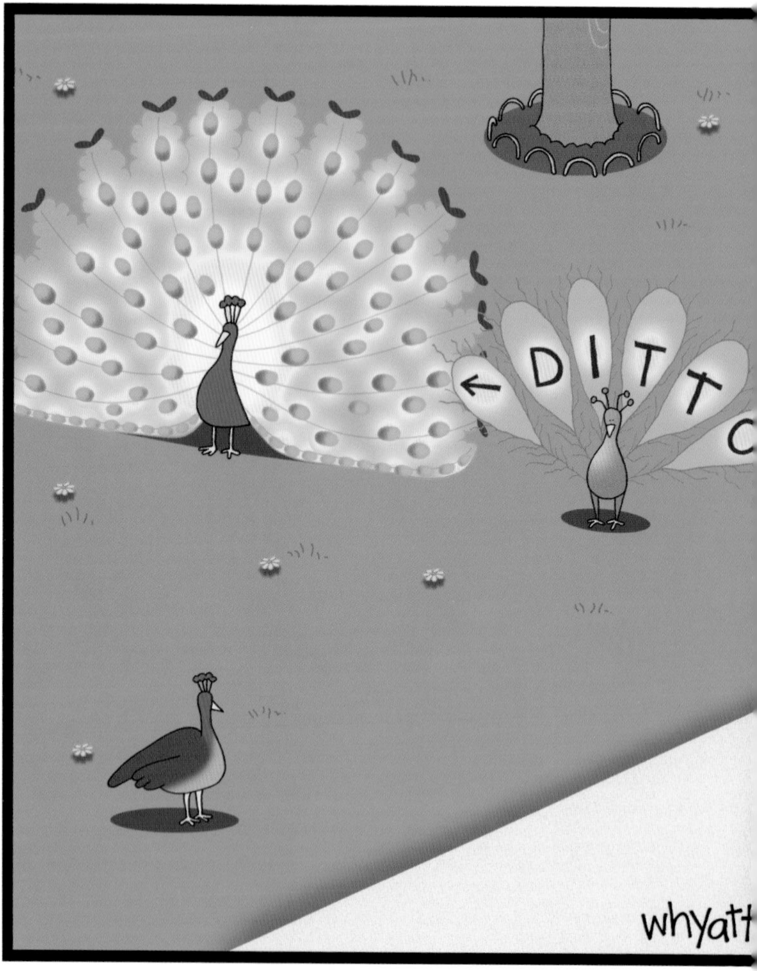

← DITTO
whyatt

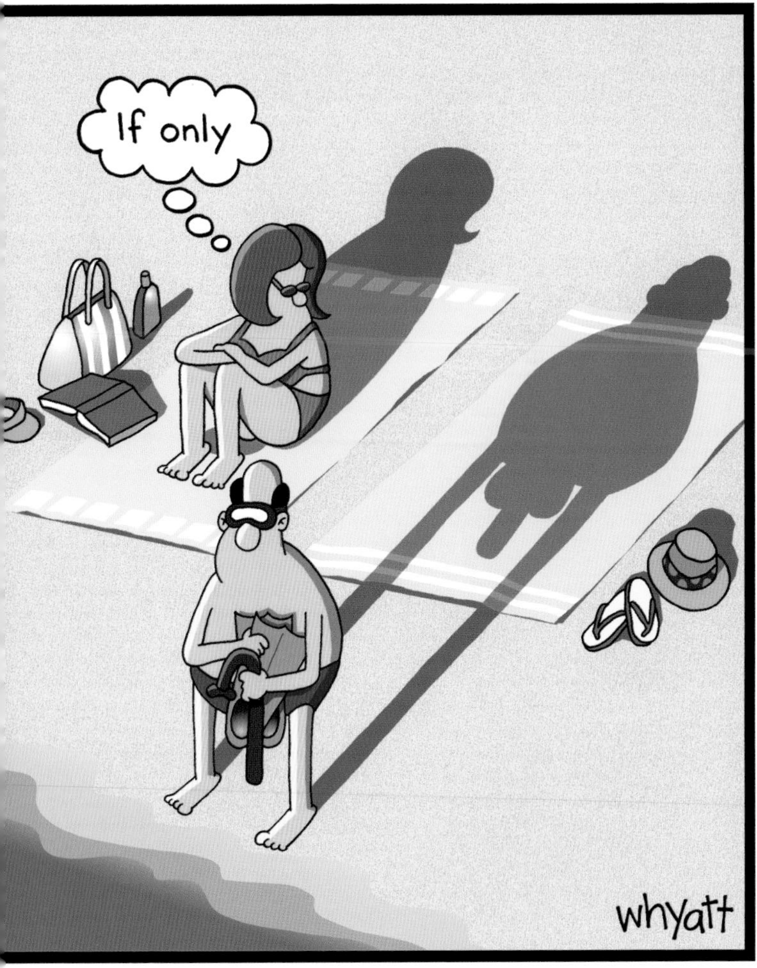
If only
whyatt

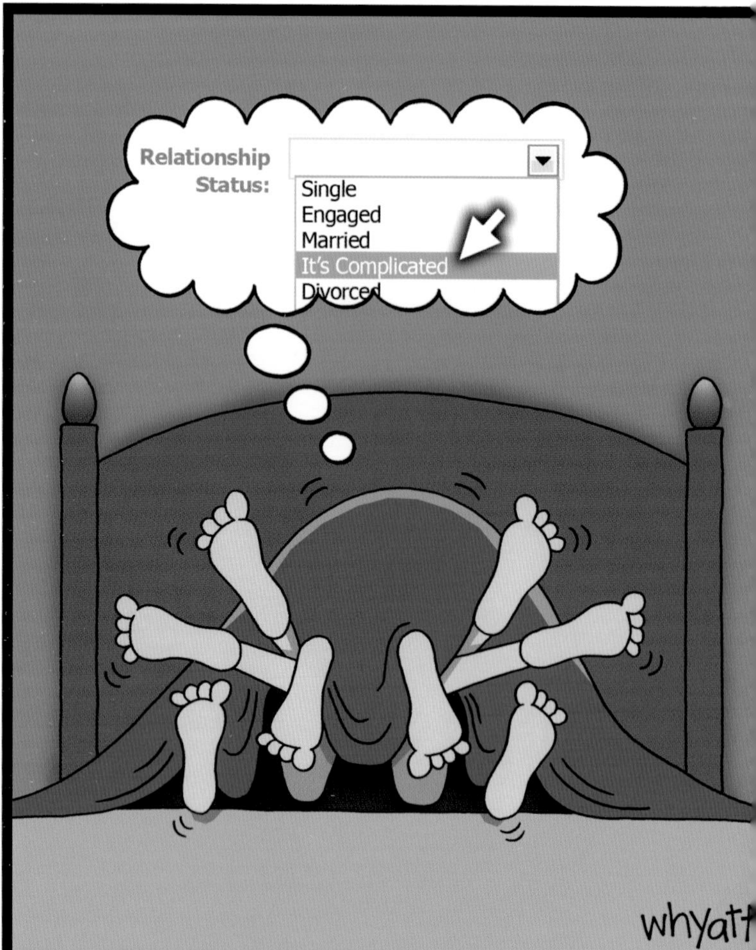
Relationship Status:
Single
Engaged
Married
It's Complicated
Divorced
whyatt

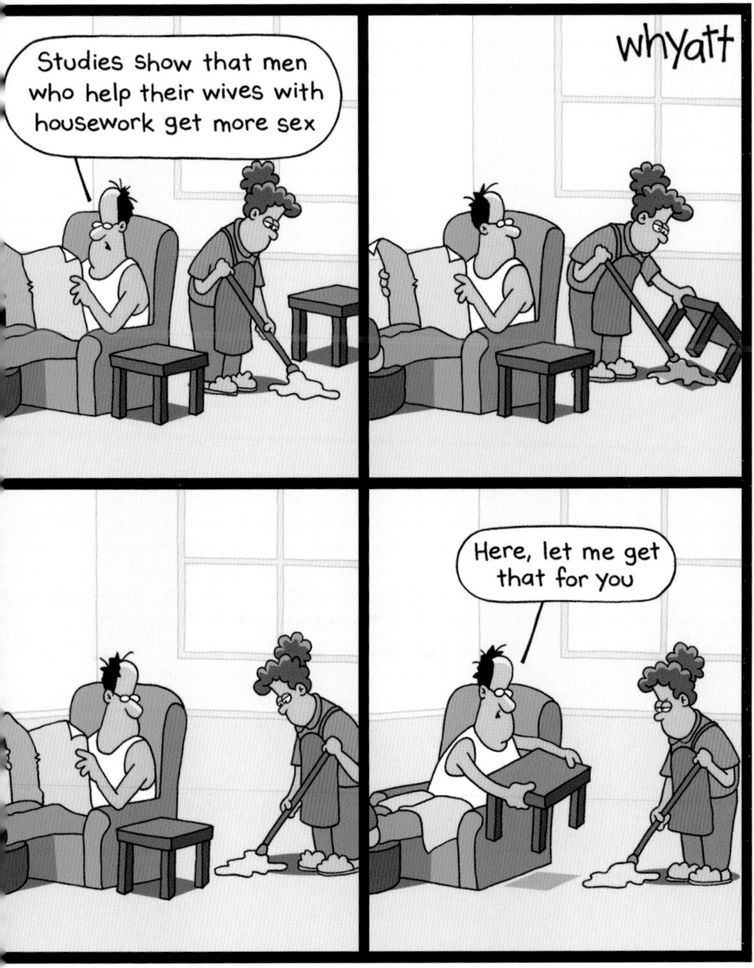
Studies show that men who help their wives with housework get more sex
whyatt
Here, let me get that for you

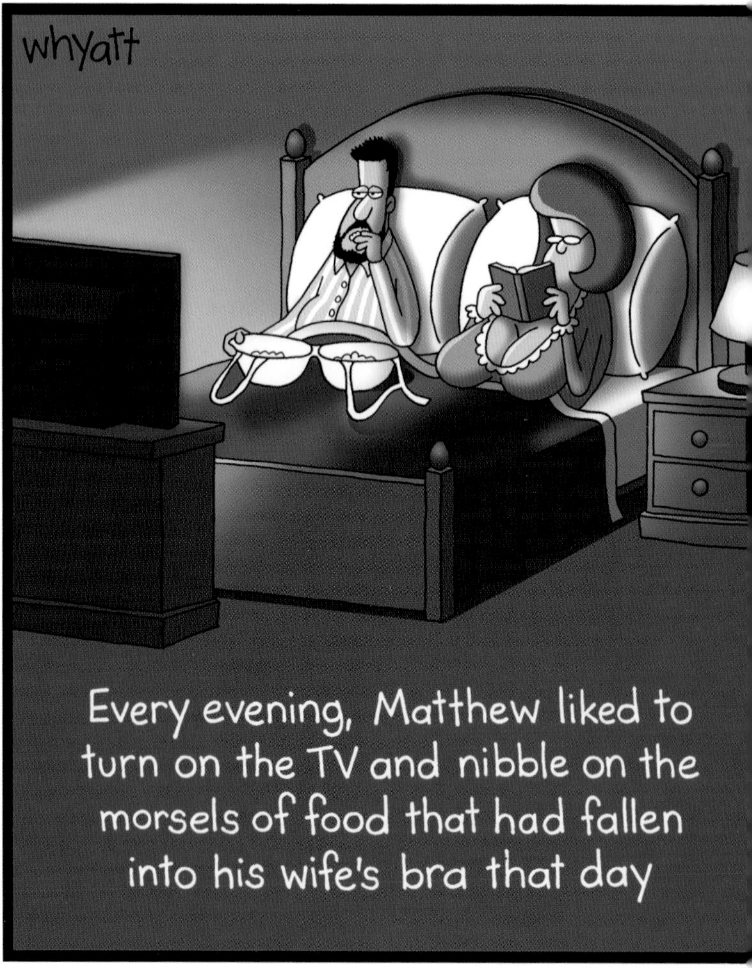
whyatt
Every evening, Matthew liked to turn on the TV and nibble on the morsels of food that had fallen into his wife's bra that day

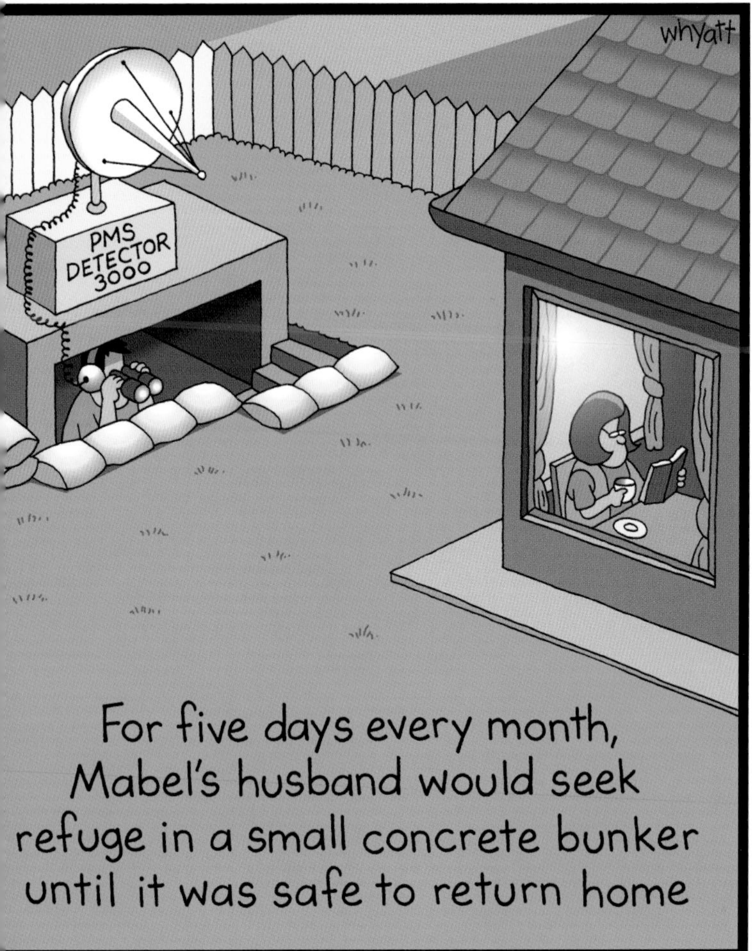
whyatt
PMS DETECTOR 3000

For five days every month, Mabel's husband would seek refuge in a small concrete bunker until it was safe to return home

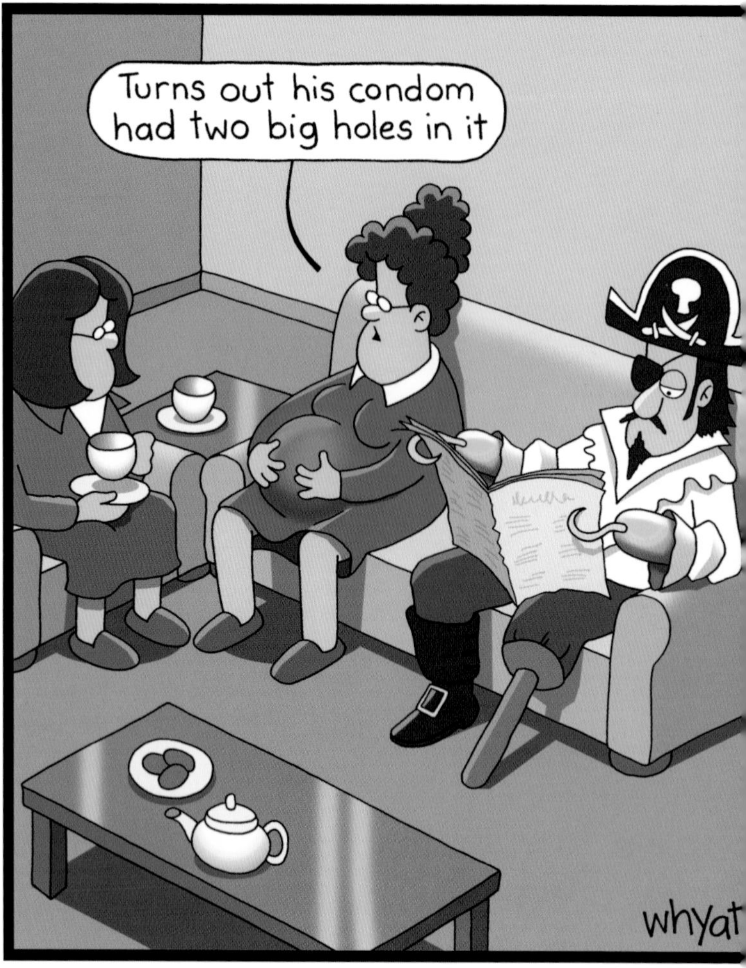
Turns out his condom had two big holes in it
whyat

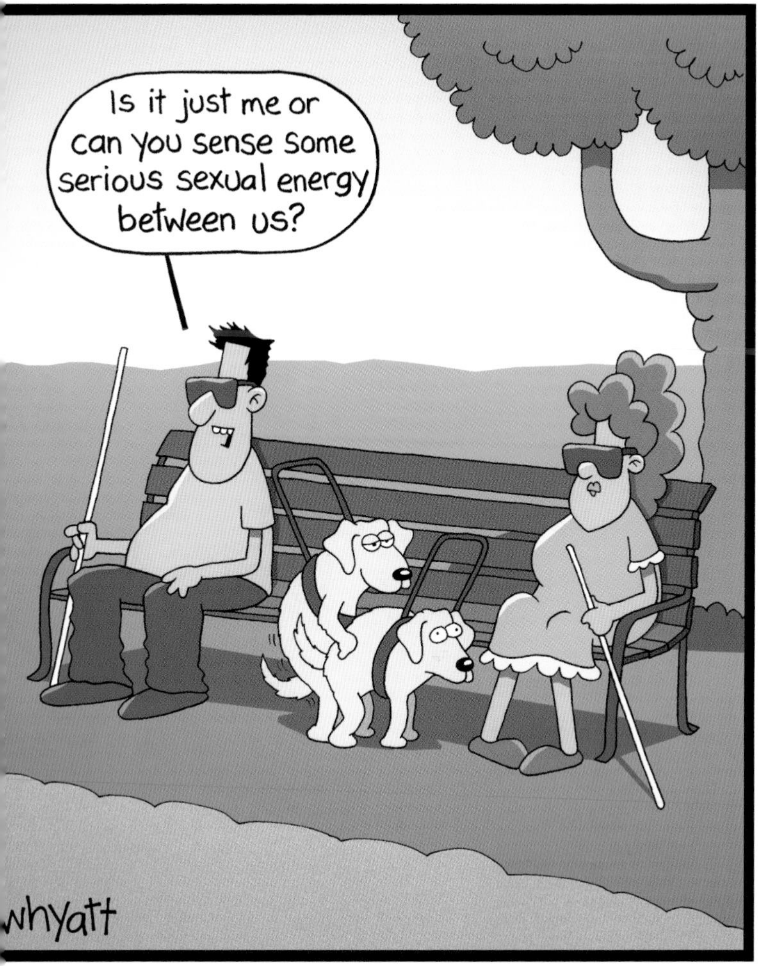
Is it just me or can you sense some serious sexual energy between us?
whyatt

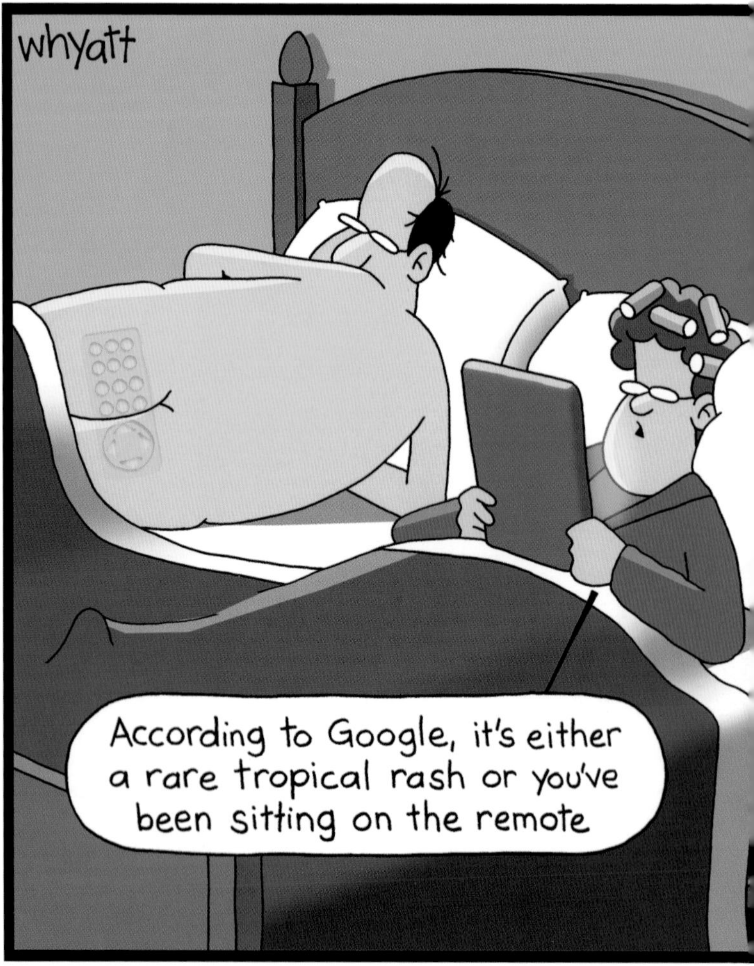
whyatt
According to Google, it's either a rare tropical rash or you've been sitting on the remote

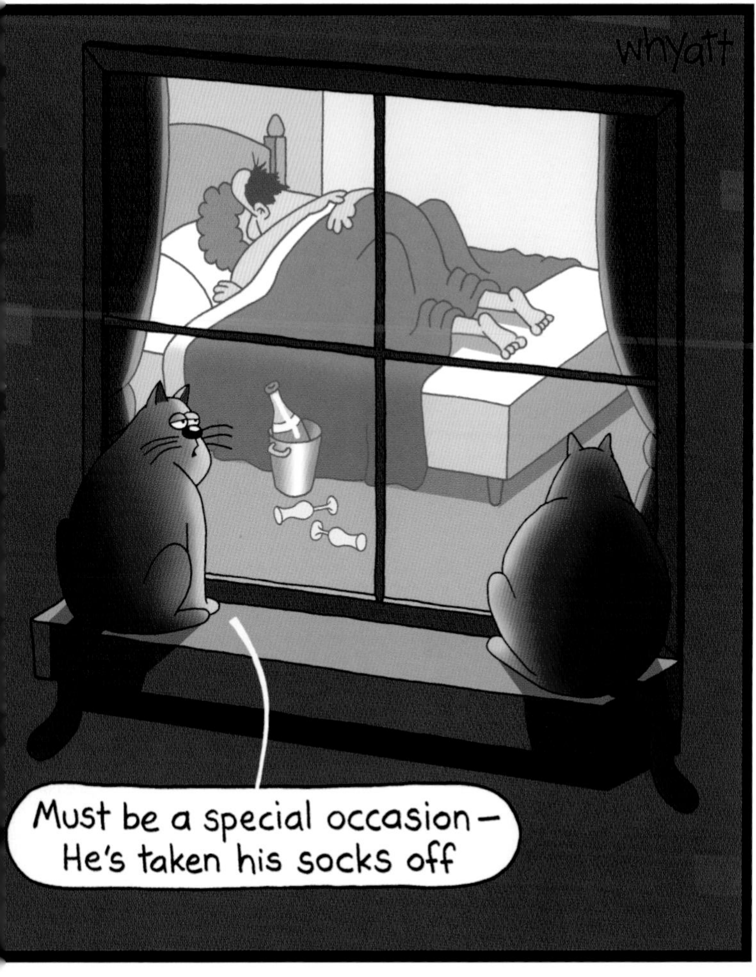
whyatt
Must be a special occasion – He's taken his socks off

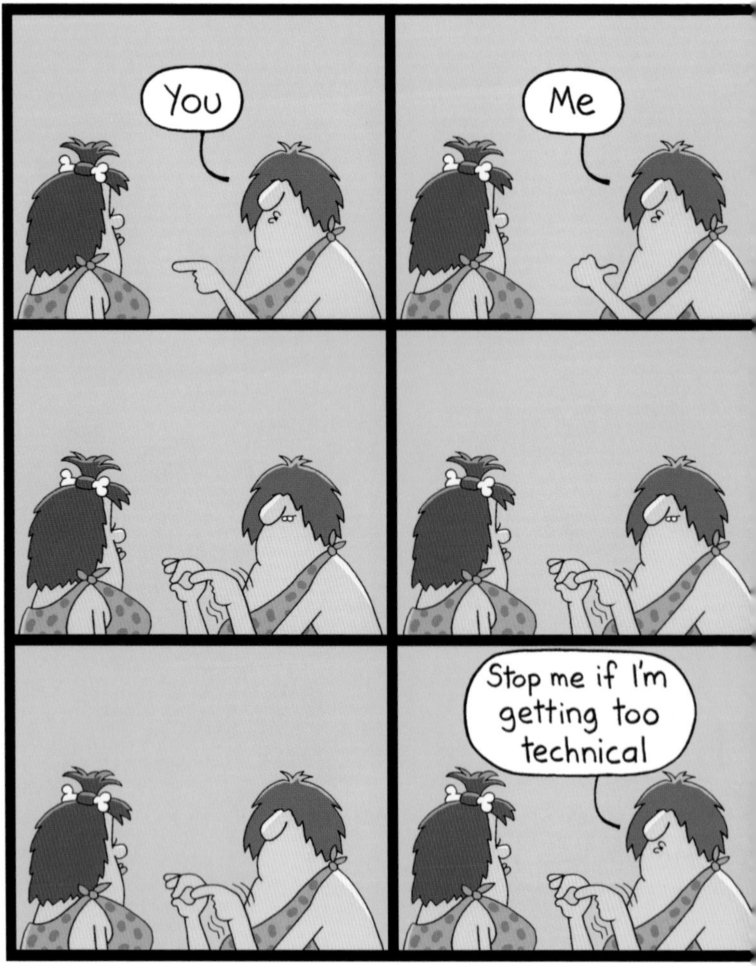
You
Me
Stop me if I'm getting too technical

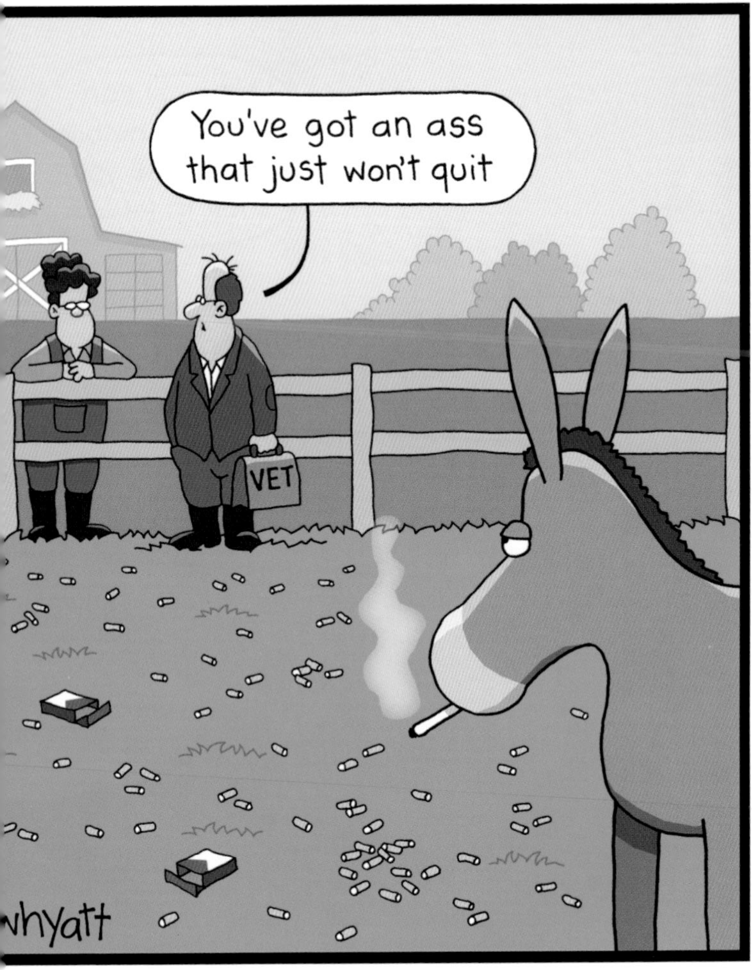
You've got an ass that just won't quit
VET
whyatt

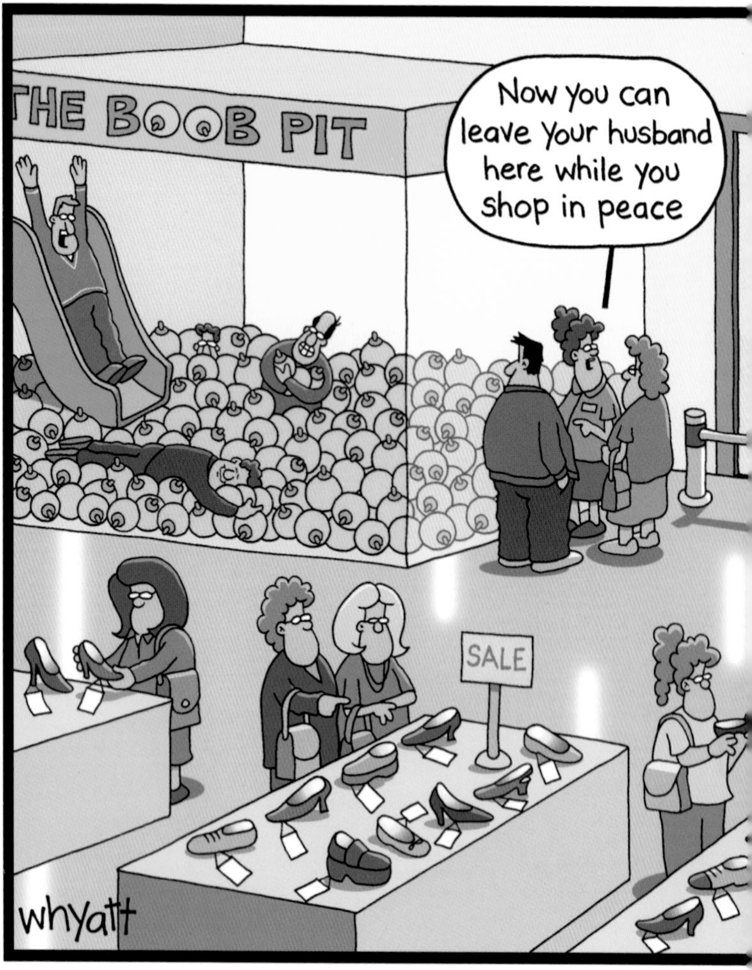
THE BOOB PIT
Now you can leave your husband here while you shop in peace
SALE
whyatt

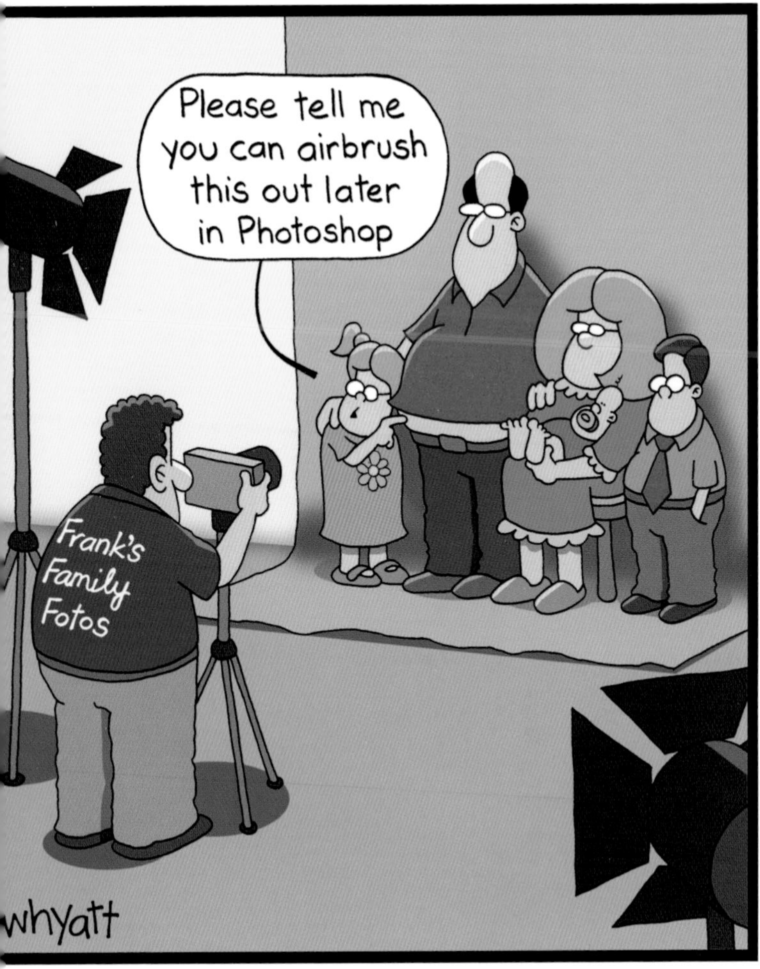
Please tell me you can airbrush this out later in Photoshop
Frank's Family Fotos
whyatt

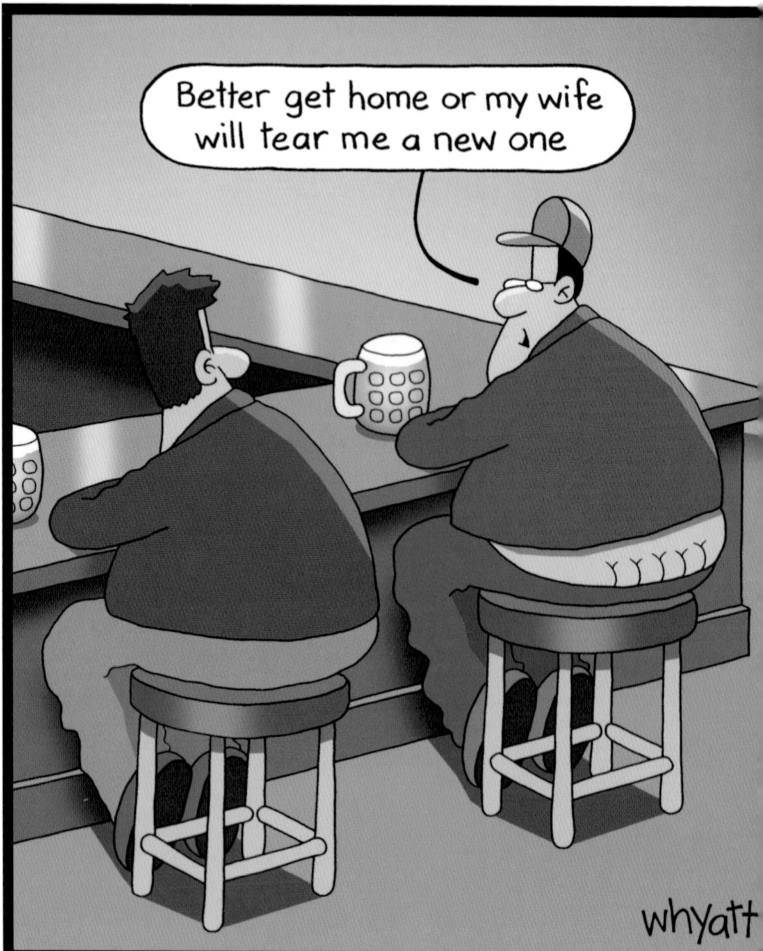
Better get home or my wife will tear me a new one
whyatt

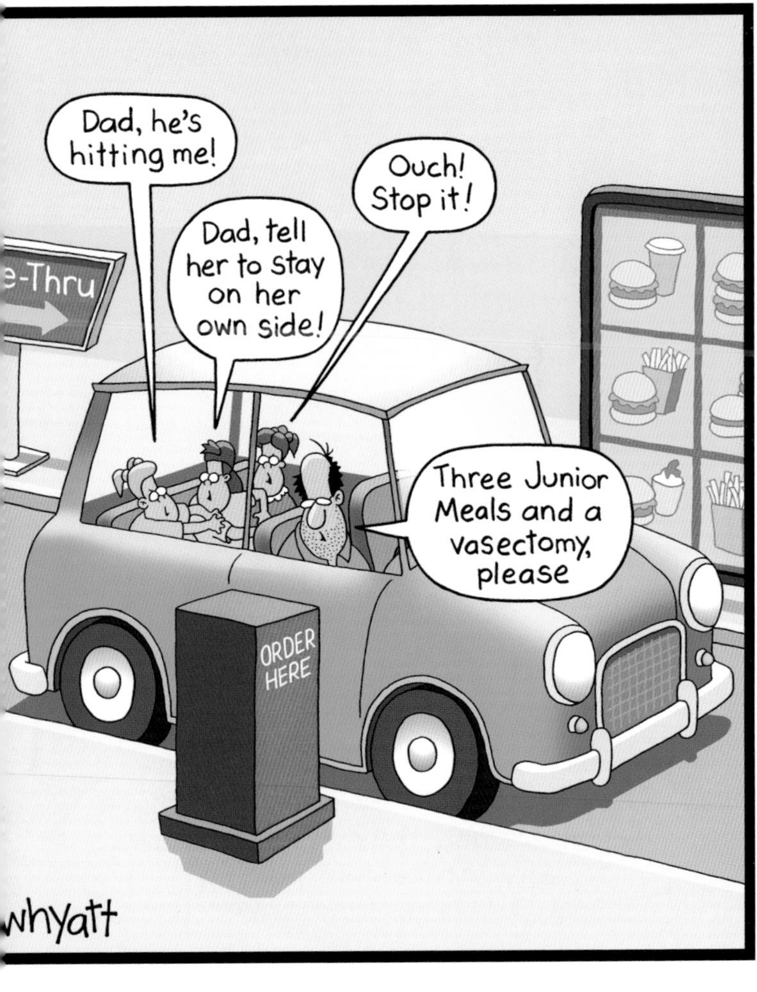
Dad, he's hitting me!
Ouch! Stop it!
Dad, tell her to stay on her own side!
e-Thru
Three Junior Meals and a vasectomy, please
ORDER HERE
whyatt

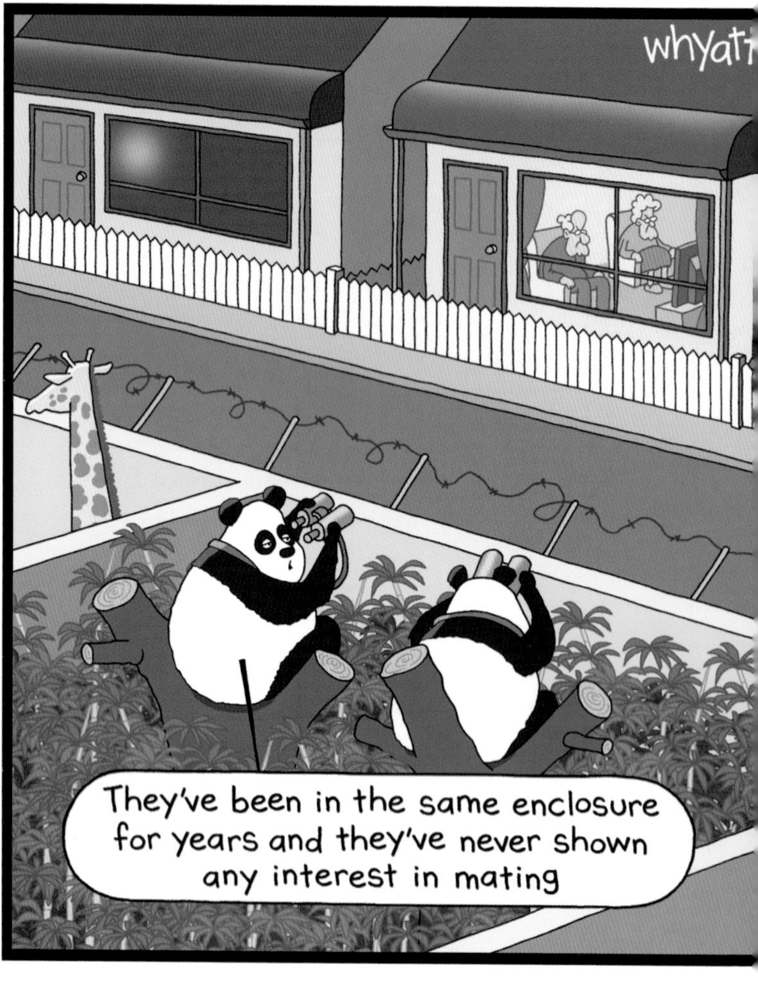
whyatt
They've been in the same enclosure for years and they've never shown any interest in mating

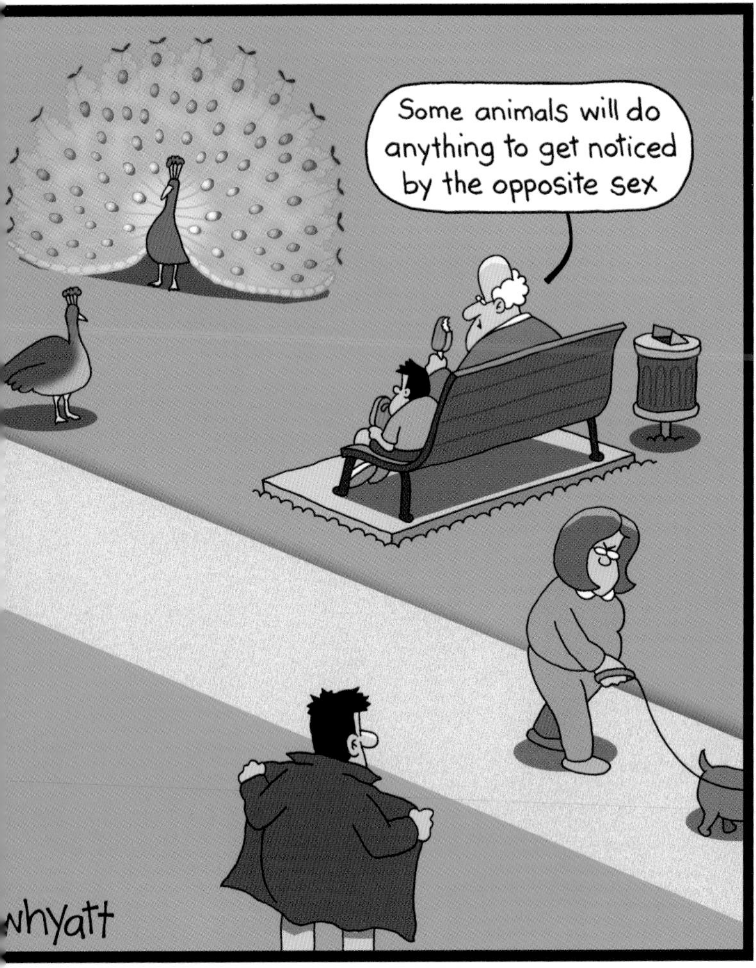
Some animals will do anything to get noticed by the opposite sex
whyatt

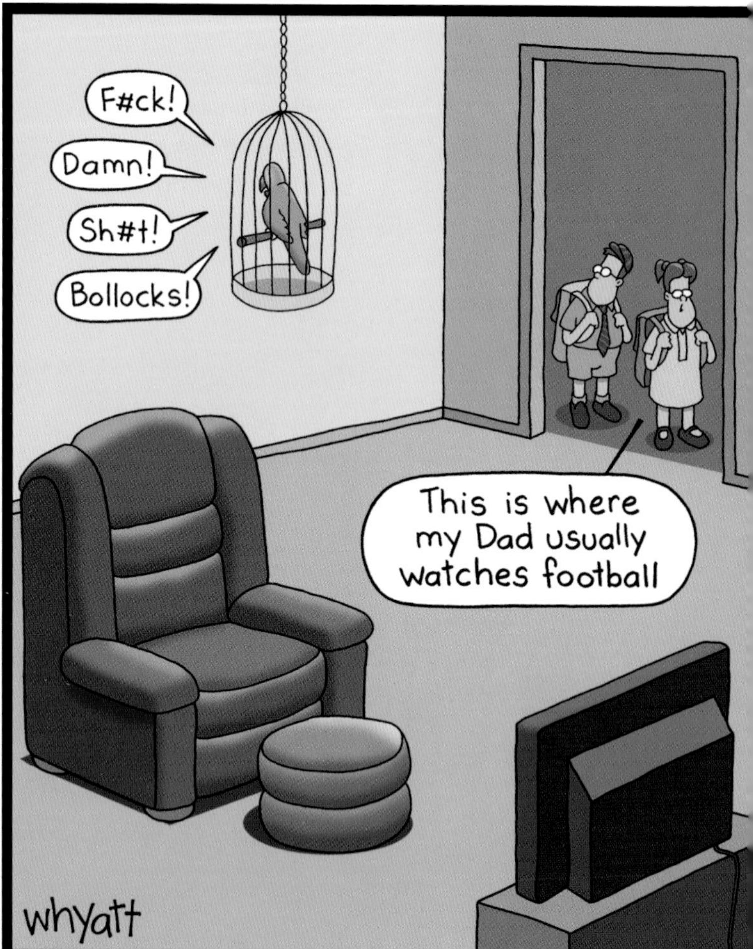
F#ck!
Damn!
Sh#t!
Bollocks!
This is where my Dad usually watches football
whyatt

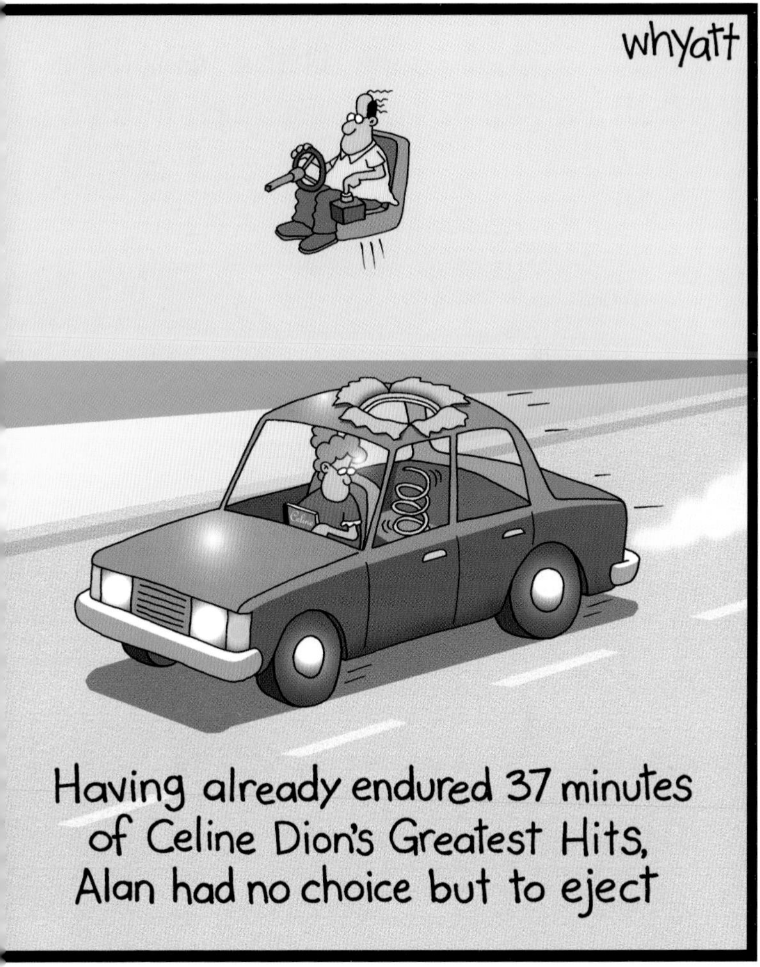
whyatt

Having already endured 37 minutes of Celine Dion's Greatest Hits, Alan had no choice but to eject

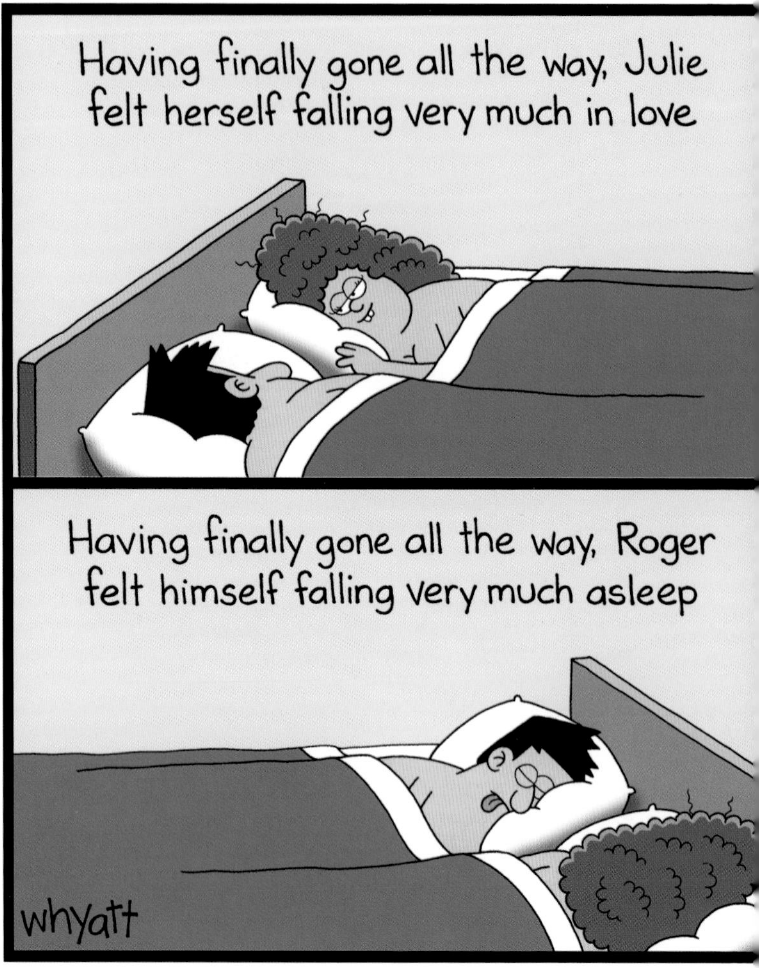
Having finally gone all the way, Julie felt herself falling very much in love
Having finally gone all the way, Roger felt himself falling very much asleep
whyatt

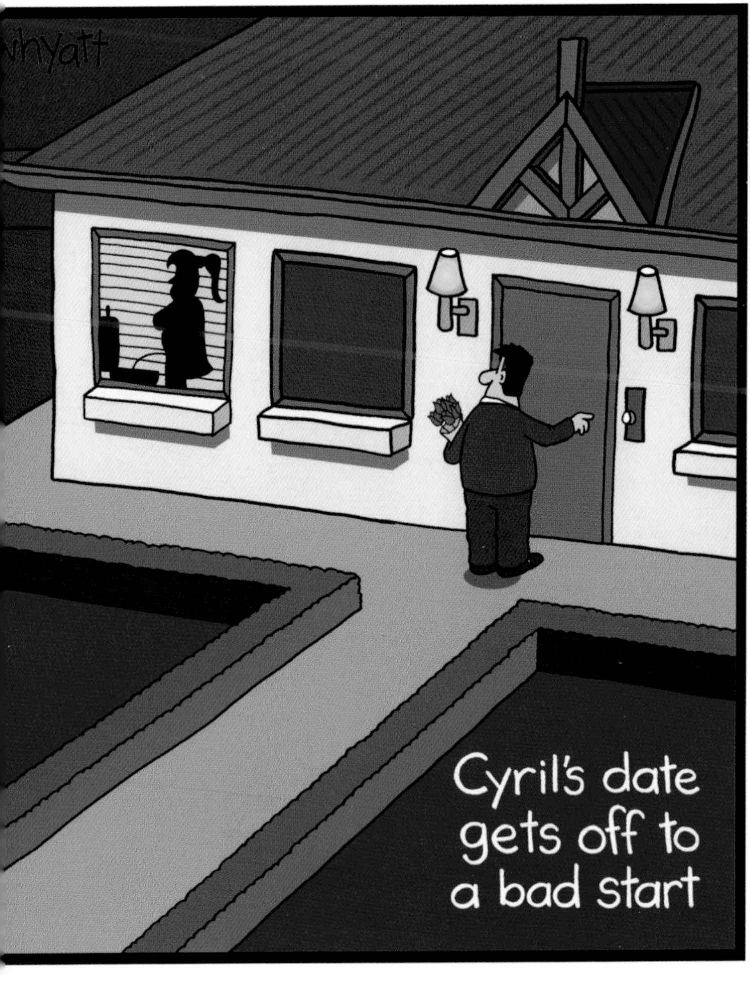
hyatt
Cyril's date
gets off to
a bad start

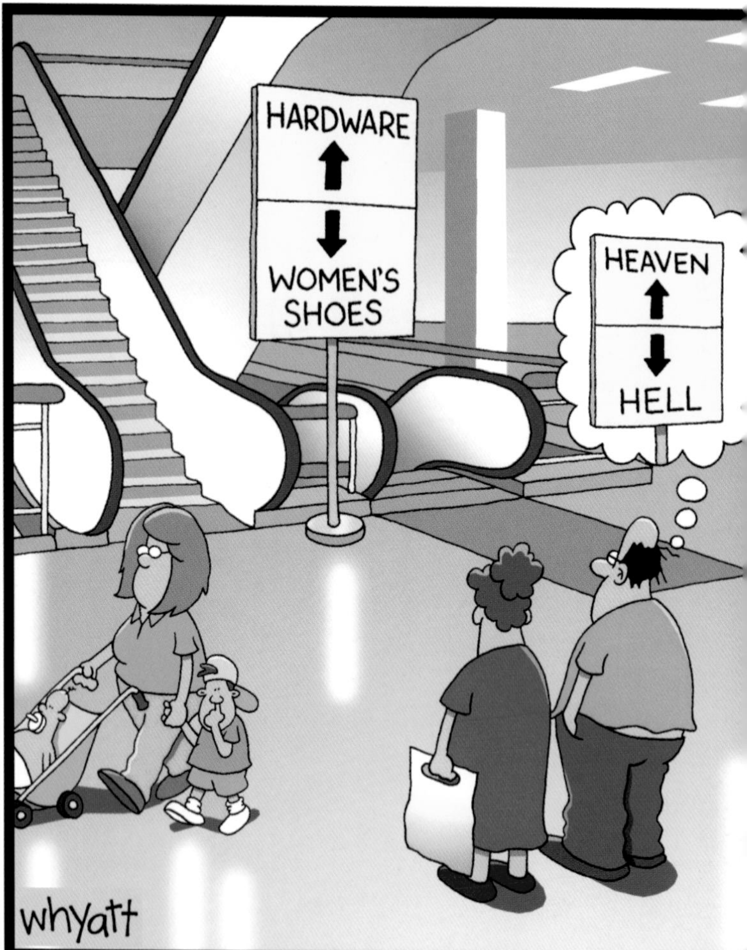
HARDWARE
WOMEN'S SHOES
HEAVEN
HELL
whyatt

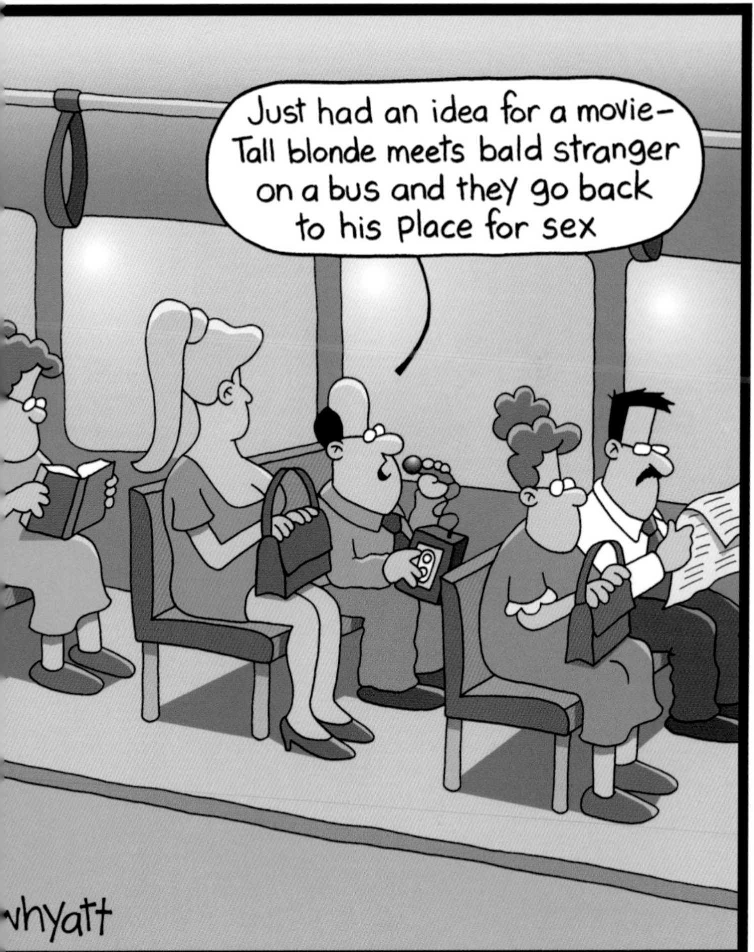
Just had an idea for a movie-
Tall blonde meets bald stranger
on a bus and they go back
to his place for sex
vhyatt

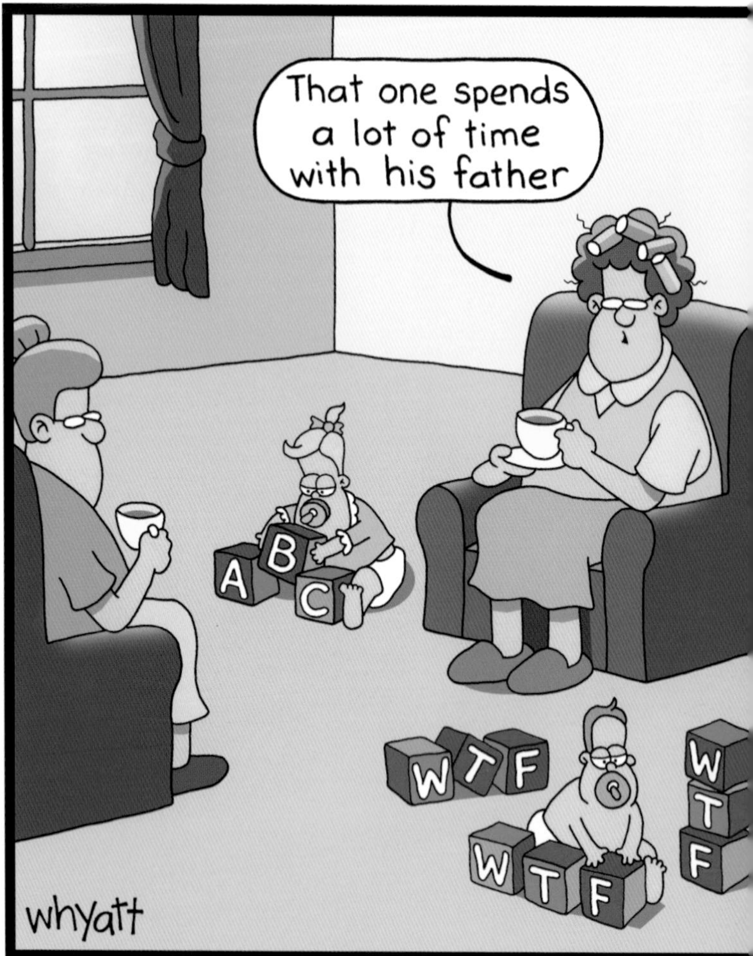
That one spends a lot of time with his father
A
B
C
W
T
F
W
T
F
W
T
F
whyatt

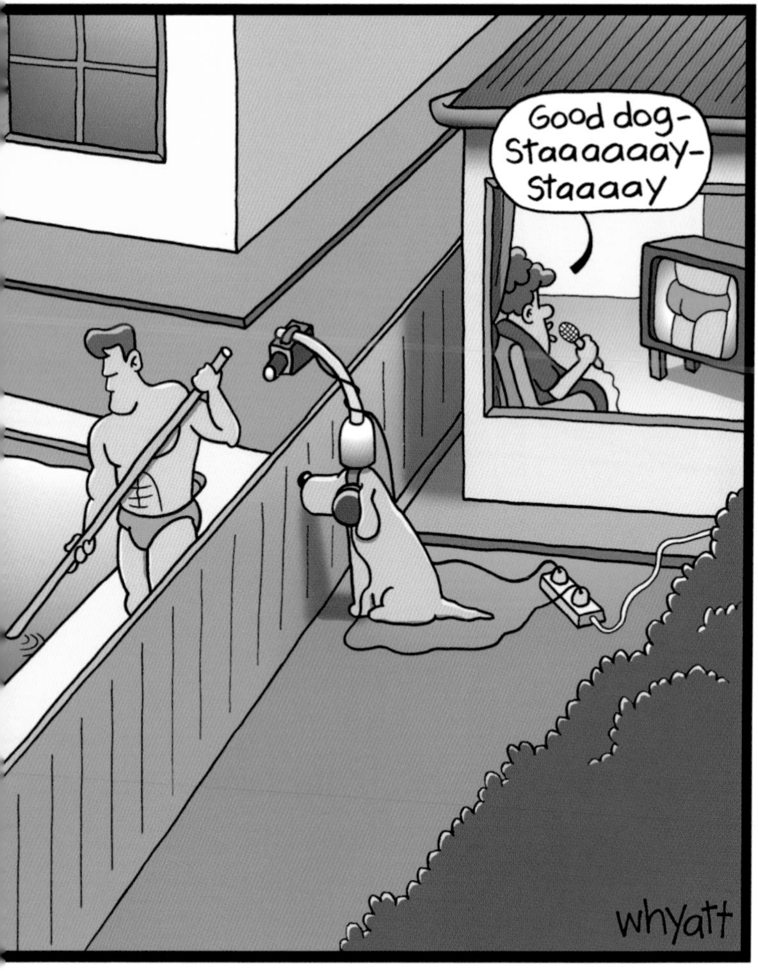
Good dog-
Staaaaaay-
Staaaay
whyatt

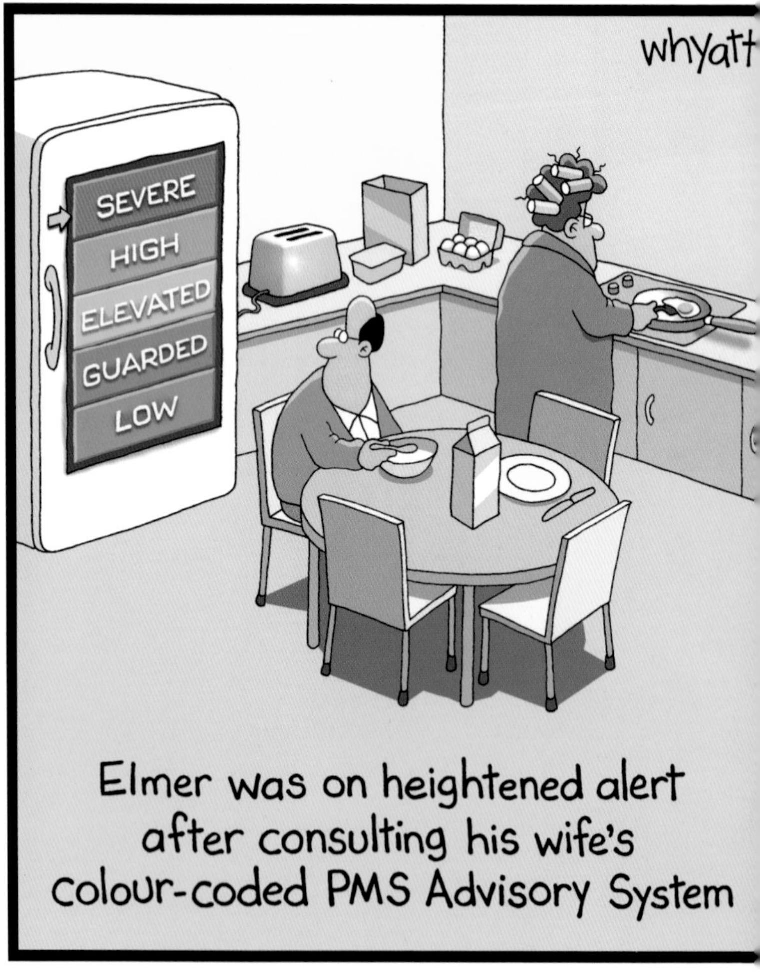
whyatt
SEVERE
HIGH
ELEVATED
GUARDED
LOW

Elmer was on heightened alert after consulting his wife's colour-coded PMS Advisory System

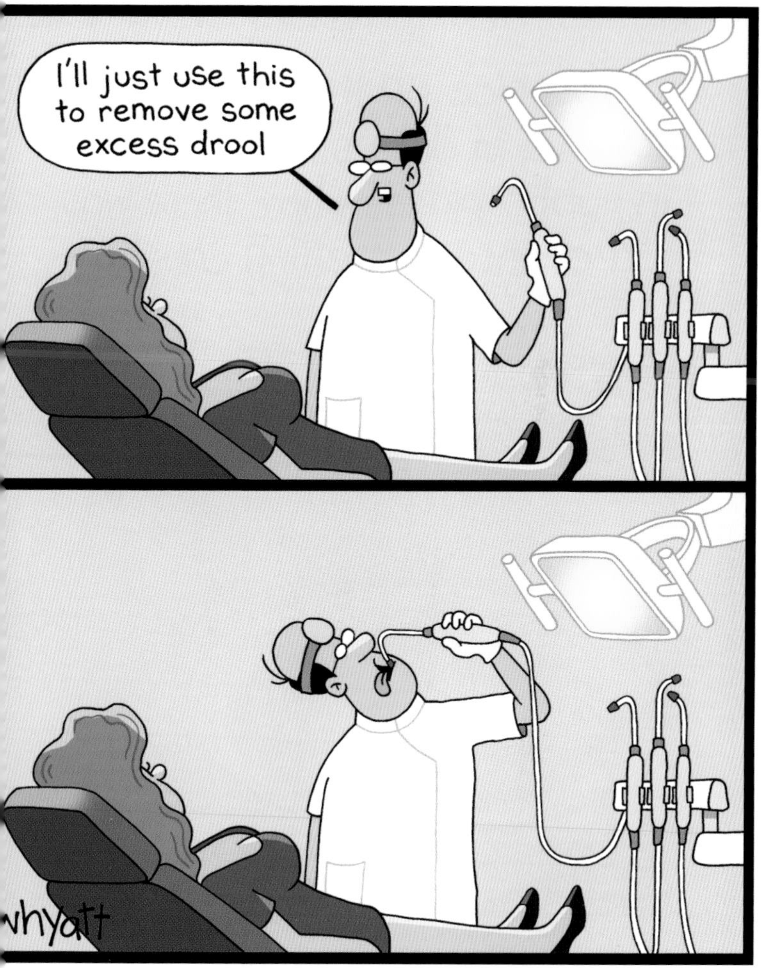
I'll just use this to remove some excess drool
whyatt

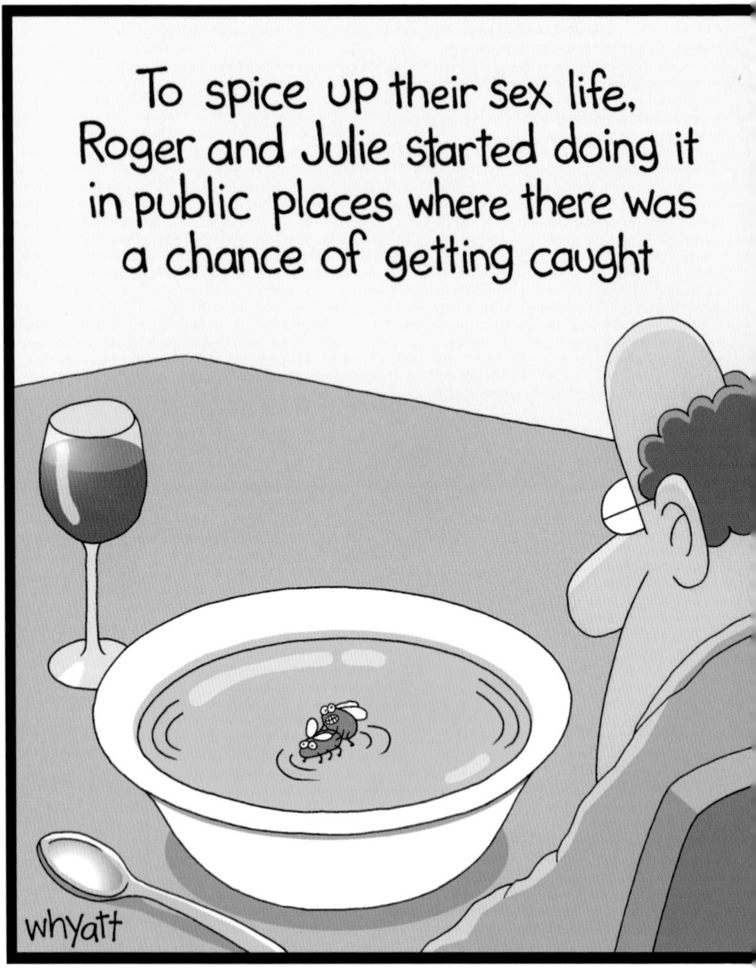
To spice up their sex life, Roger and Julie started doing it in public places where there was a chance of getting caught
whyatt

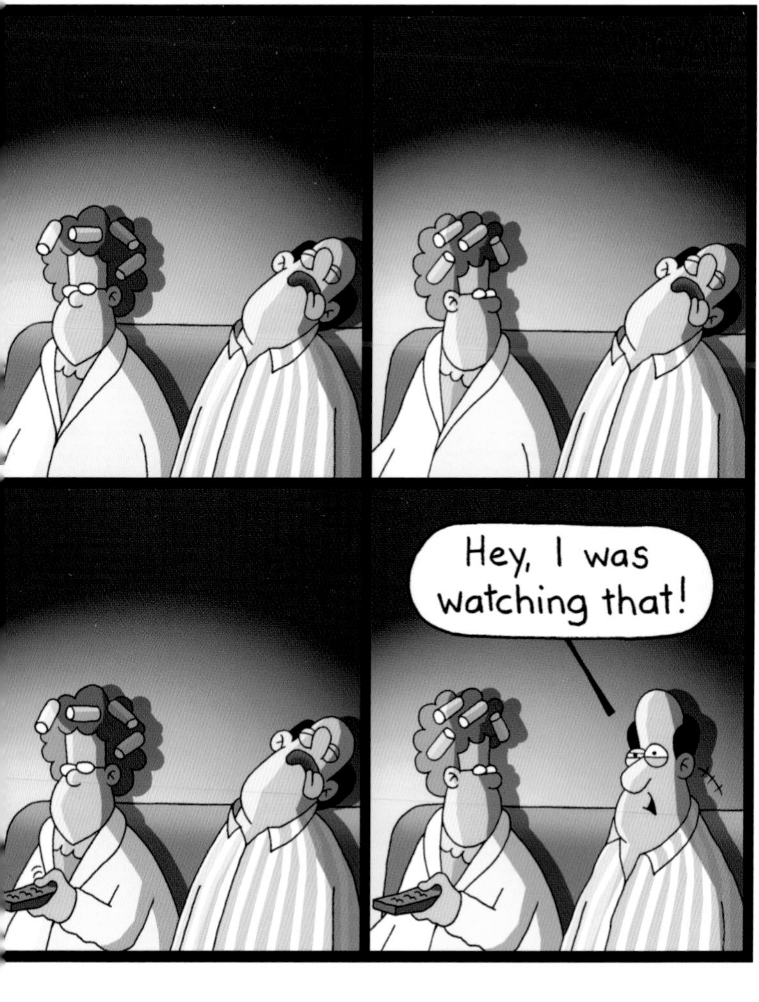
Hey, I was watching that!

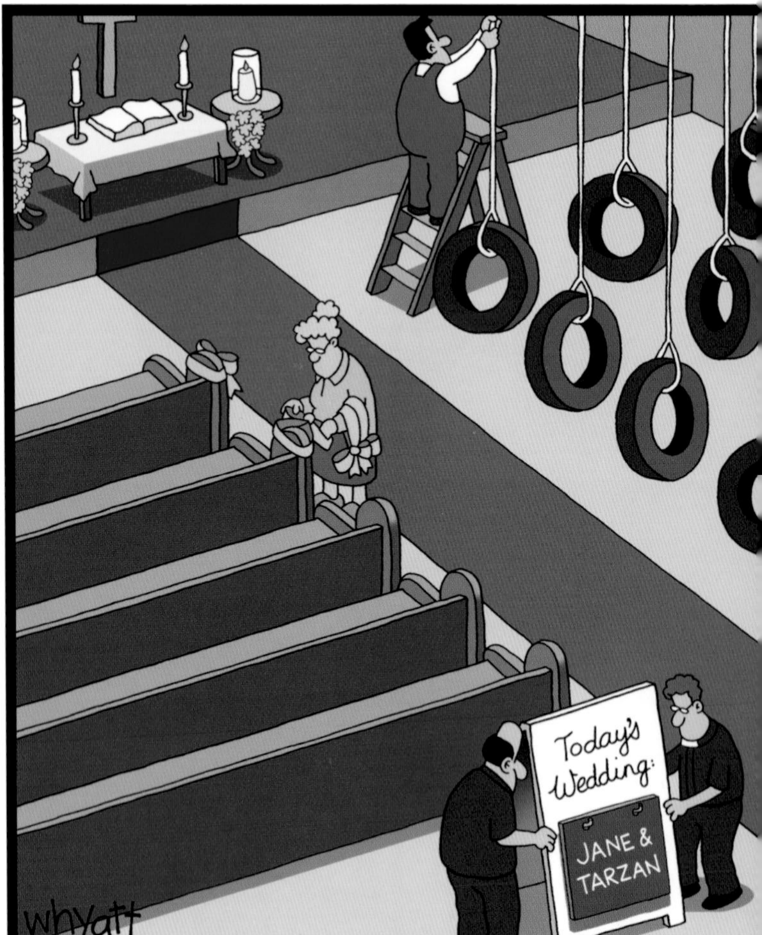

Today's Wedding:
JANE & TARZAN
whyatt

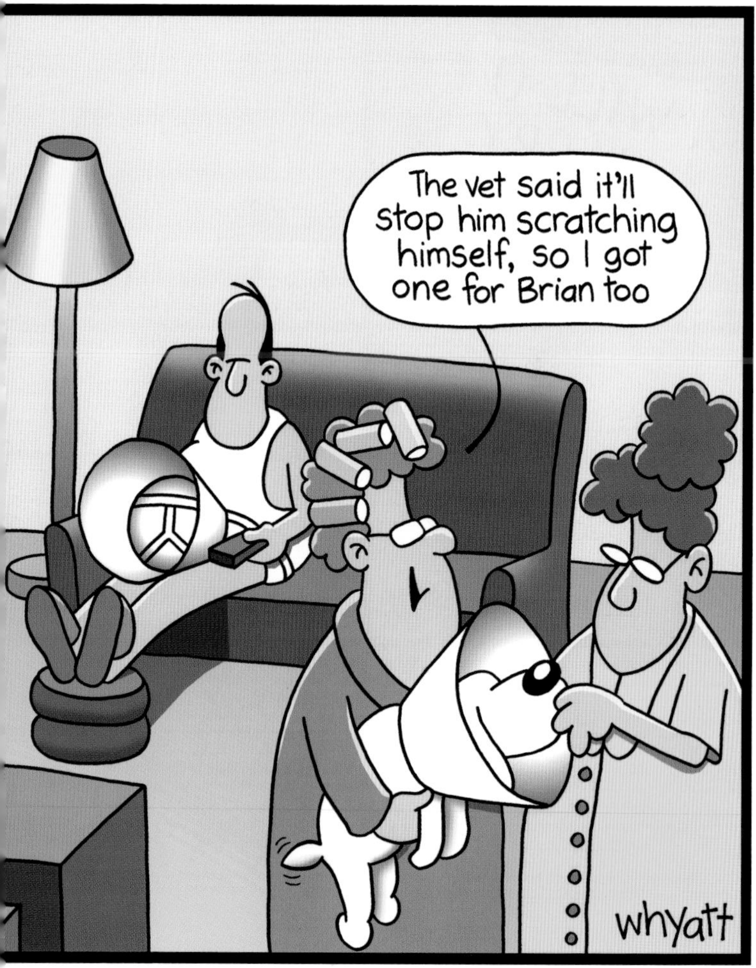
The vet said it'll stop him scratching himself, so I got one for Brian too
whyatt

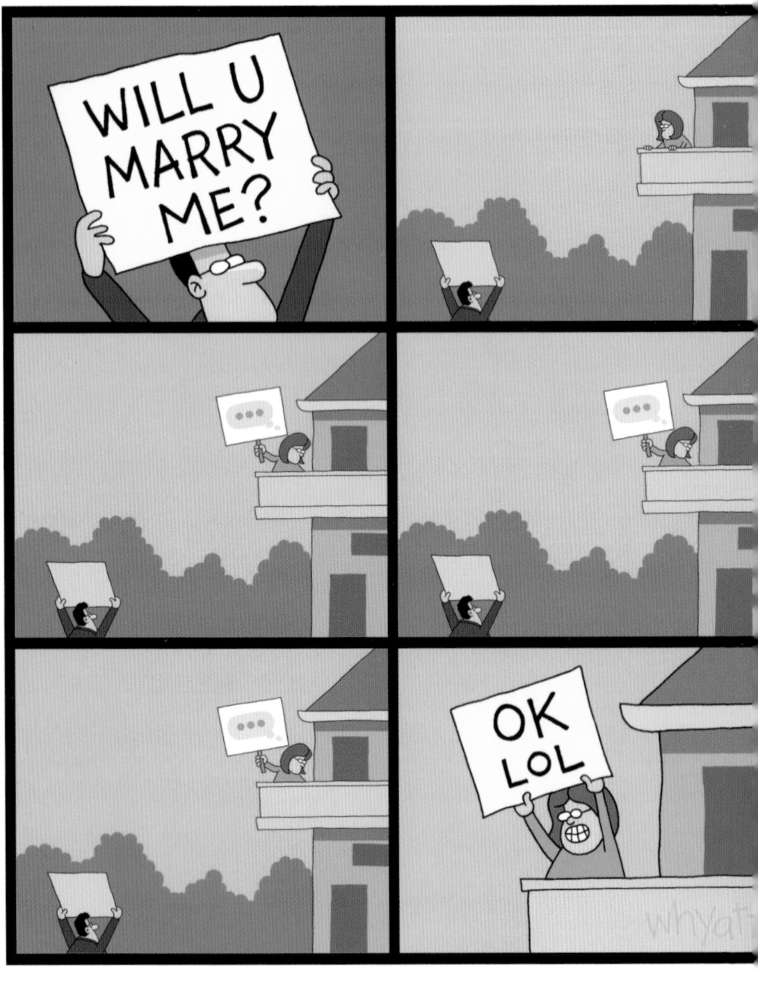
WILL U MARRY ME?
OK LOL

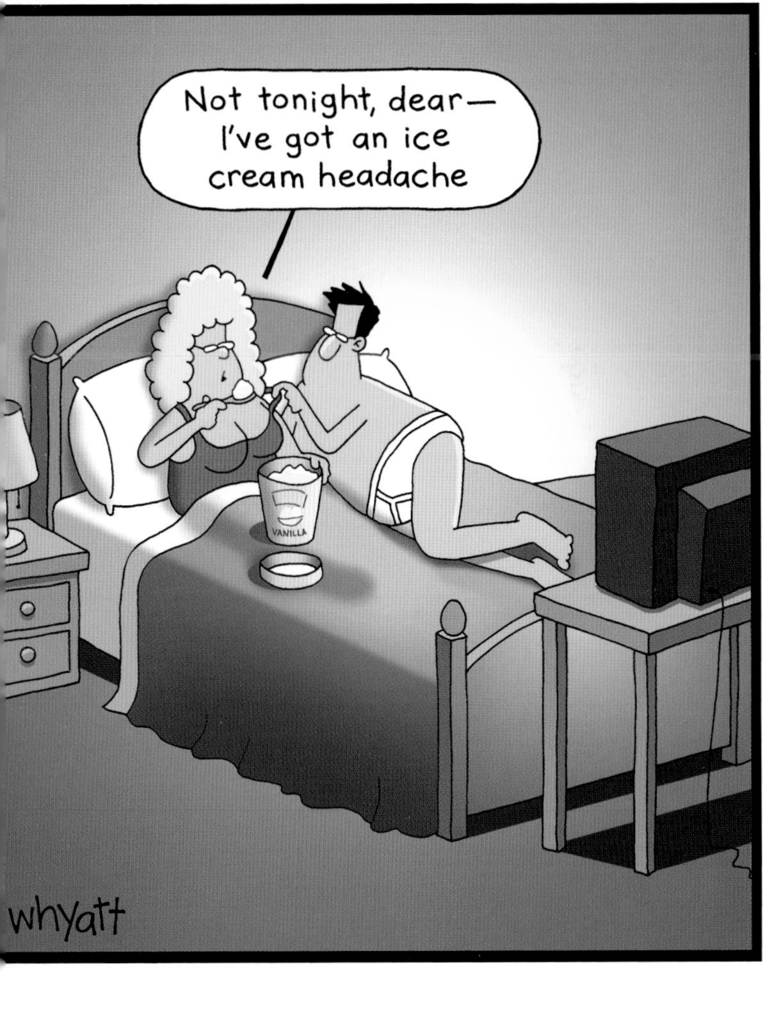
Not tonight, dear—
I've got an ice
cream headache
VANILLA
whyatt

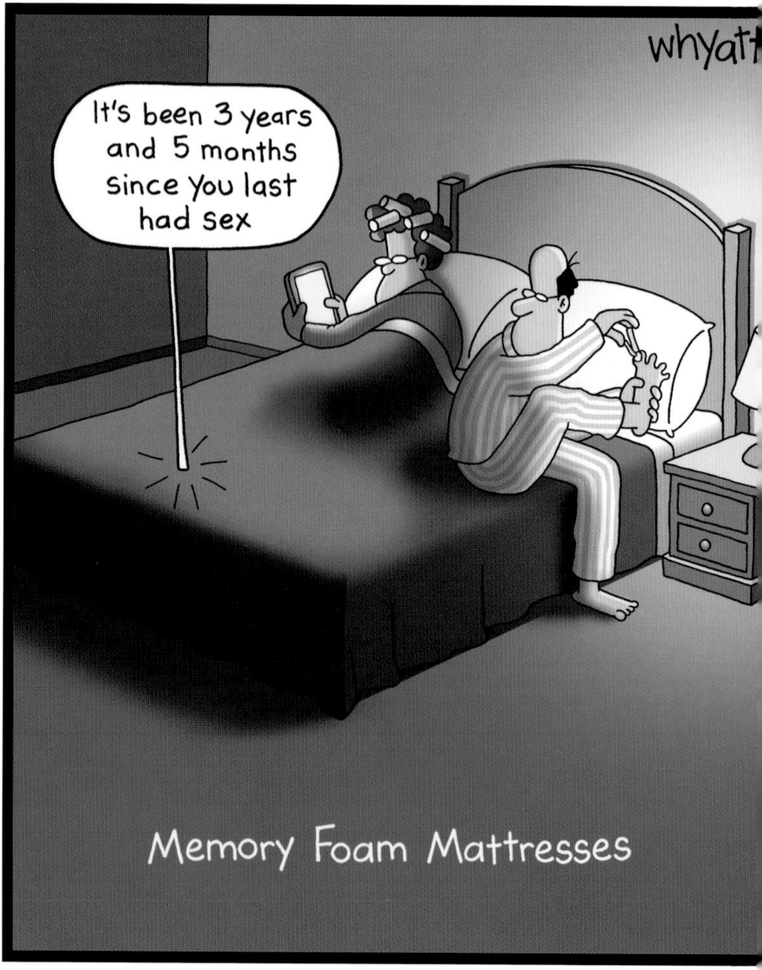
whyatt
It's been 3 years and 5 months since you last had sex
Memory Foam Mattresses

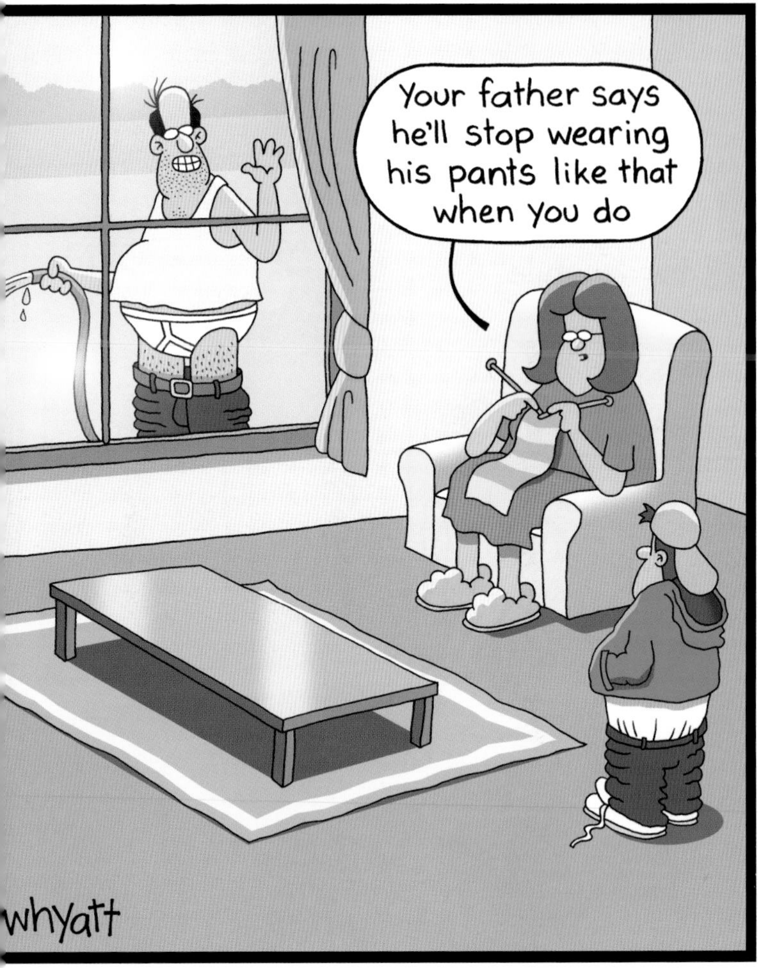
Your father says he'll stop wearing his pants like that when you do
whyatt

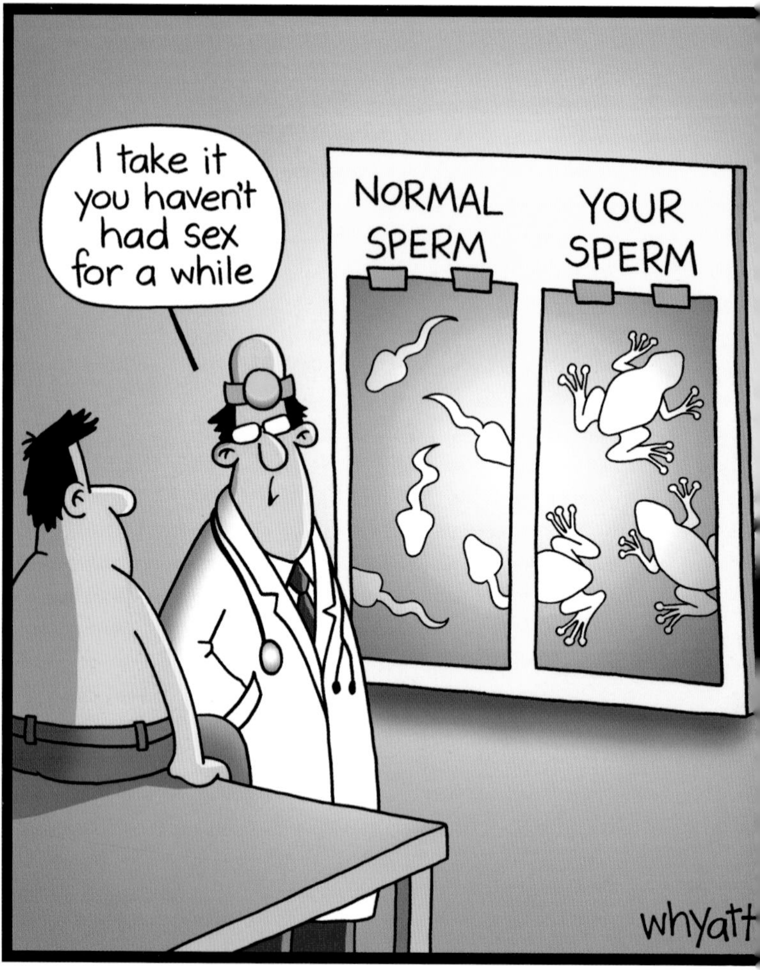
I take it you haven't had sex for a while
NORMAL SPERM
YOUR SPERM
whyatt

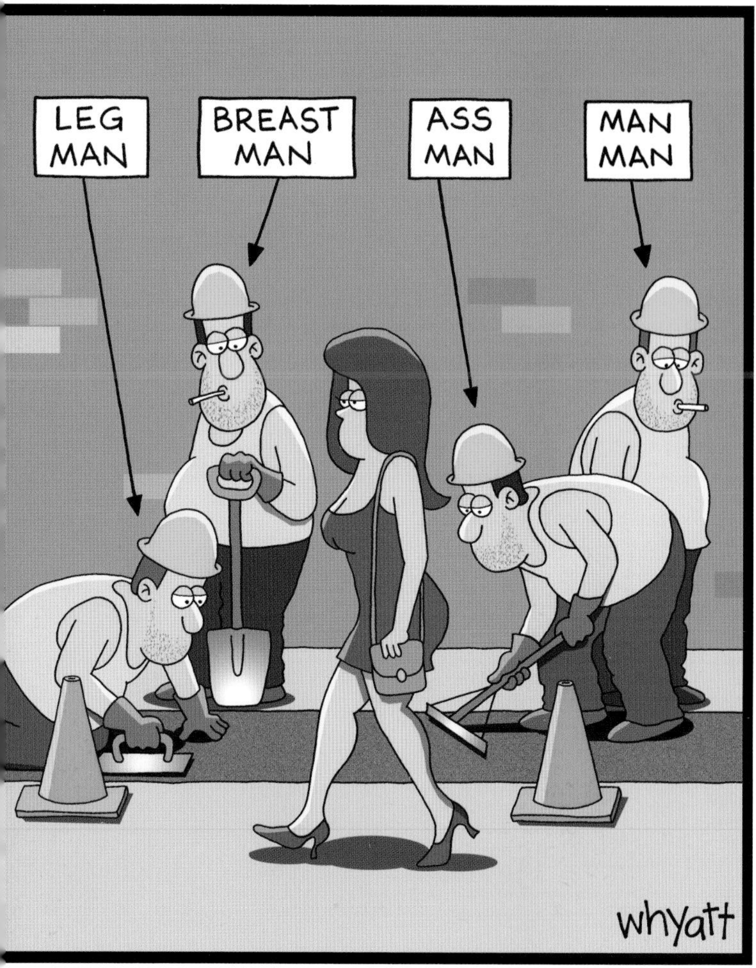
LEG MAN
BREAST MAN
ASS MAN
MAN MAN
whyatt

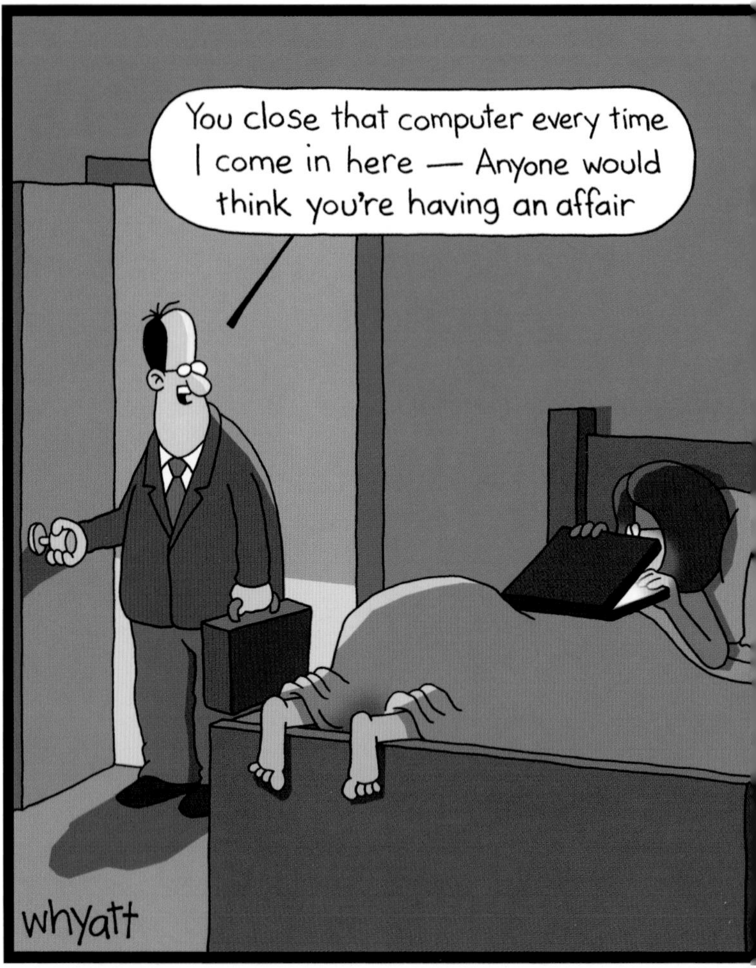
You close that computer every time I come in here — Anyone would think you're having an affair
whyatt

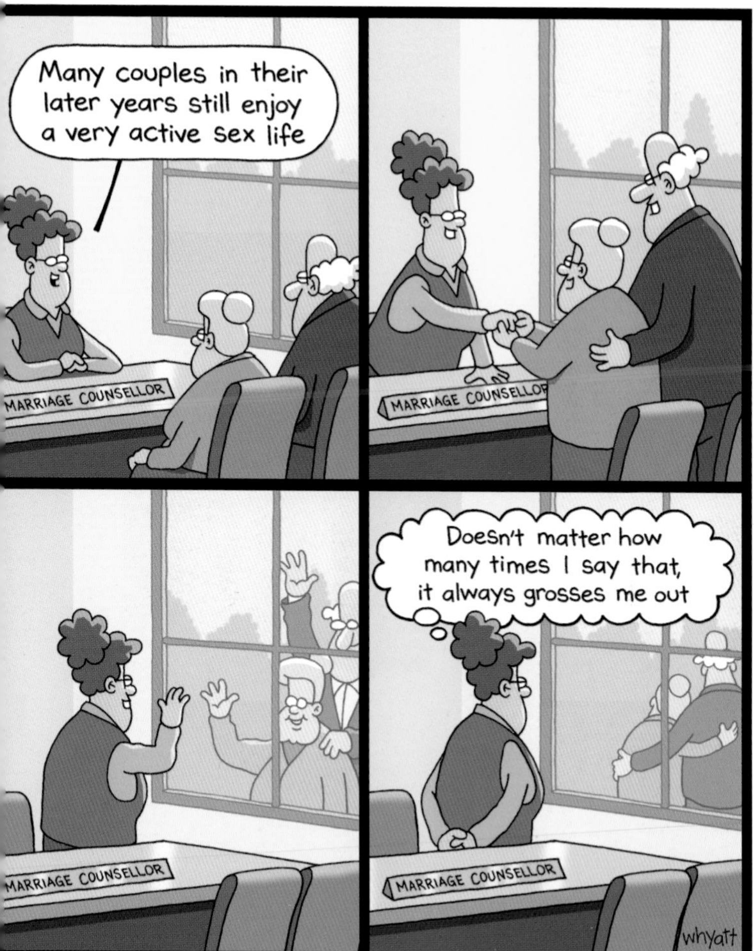
Many couples in their later years still enjoy a very active sex life
MARRIAGE COUNSELLOR
MARRIAGE COUNSELLOR
MARRIAGE COUNSELLOR
Doesn't matter how many times I say that, it always grosses me out
MARRIAGE COUNSELLOR
whyatt